W9-BLR-574

Chicago Public Library
Oriole Park Branch
7454 W. Balmoral Ave.
Chicago, IL 60656

DISCARD

EXPLORING SCIENCE

# FORCE AND MOTION

### LAWS OF MOVEMENT

#### BY DON NARDO

Content Adviser: Steven Shropshire, Ph.D.,
Department of Physics, Idaho State University

Science Adviser: Terrence E. Young Jr., M.Ed., M.L.S.,
Jefferson Parish (Louisiana) Public School System

Reading Adviser: Rosemary G. Palmer, Ph.D., Department of Literacy,
College of Education, Boise State University

 Compass Point Books · Minneapolis, Minnesota

Compass Point Books • 3109 West 50th Street, #115 • Minneapolis, MN 55410

Visit Compass Point Books on the Internet at *www.compasspointbooks.com*
or e-mail your request to *custserv@compasspointbooks.com*

Photographs ©: George B. Diebold/Corbis, cover; Jeff Greenberg/Peter Arnold, Inc., 4; Kristian/Shutterstock, 5; Guy Sauvage/Photo Researchers, Inc., 6; Craig Hansen/Shutterstock, 7; Susana Vera/Reuters/Corbis, 9; Patrick Hermans/Shutterstock, 10; The Granger Collection, New York, 11, 13; Erich Lessing/Art Resource, NY, 12; Courtesy History of Science Collections, University of Oklahoma Libraries, copyright the Board of Regents of the University, 14; Bildarchiv Preussischer Kulturbesitz/Art Resource, NY, 15; Jeff Metzger/Shutterstock, 17; Ariel Bravy/Shutterstock, 18; Iztok Noc/Shutterstock, 19; Crown Copyright/Health & Safety Laboratory/Photo Researchers, Inc., 21; Karina Maybely Orellana Rojas/Shutterstock, 22; Aleksandrs Marinicevs/Shutterstock, 23; Peter Frischmuth/Peter Arnold, Inc., 24; Dr. Morley Read/Photo Researchers, Inc., 25; Comstock Images, 26; Photodisc, 27; Charles Taylor/Shutterstock, 28; George Steinmetz/Corbis, 29; Andrew Lambert Photography/Photo Researchers, Inc., 30; David Woods/Corbis, 33; Jason Maehl/Shutterstock, 34; Nick Poling/Shutterstock, 35; Ilya D. Gridnev/Shutterstock, 38; A. L. Spangler/Shutterstock, 39; André Klaassen/Shutterstock, 40; Robert Kyllo/Shutterstock, 42; Manfred Kage/Peter Arnold, Inc., 43; Robert/Shutterstock, 44; Photobar/Shutterstock, 46.

Editor: Anthony Wacholtz
Designer: The Design Lab
Page Production: Lori Bye
Photo Researcher: Lori Bye
Illustrator: Ashlee Schultz

Art Director: Jaime Martens
Creative Director: Keith Griffin
Editorial Director: Nick Healy
Managing Editor: Catherine Neitge

**Library of Congress Cataloging-in-Publication Data**
Nardo, Don, 1947–
    Force and motion : laws of movement / by Don Nardo ; illustrator, Ashlee Schultz.
        p. cm.—(Exploring science)
    ISBN-13: 978-0-7565-3264-2 (library binding)
    ISBN-10: 0-7565-3264-7 (library binding)
    1. Force and energy. 2. Motion. I. Schultz, Ashlee, ill. II. Title.

    QC73.4.N365 2008
    531'.6—dc22                                                2007004604

Copyright© 2008 by Compass Point Books
All rights reserved. No part of this book may be reproduced without written permission from the publisher. The publisher takes no responsibility for the use of any of the materials or methods described in this book, nor for the products thereof.
    Printed in the United States of America.

♻ This book was manufactured with paper containing at least 10 percent post-consumer waste.

About the Author

In addition to his acclaimed volumes on ancient civilizations, historian Don Nardo has published several studies of scientific discoveries and phenomena, as well as scientists. Nardo lives with his wife, Christine, in Massachusetts.

R0413960166

## TABLE OF CONTENTS

Oriole Park Branch
7454 W. DISCARD
Chicago, IL 60656

# CHAPTER ONE

# Mass and Weight

**AS THEY SPEED ALONG** at thousands of miles per hour, astronauts orbiting Earth gaze out through small windows in their spacecraft. Around them, the moon, planets, and comets hurtle endlessly around the sun. Far below, Earth spins around like a giant top. Across its surface, people and animals walk, run, jump, ride, swim, or fly. Waves crash onto seashores, leaves fall from trees, and smoke rises from volcanoes.

From traffic streaming steadily down highways to Earth spinning on its axis, everything around us is constantly in motion.

These things are part of a universe that is almost always in motion. All movements happen as the result of the pushing and pulling actions of unseen forces.

## A POWERFUL INVISIBLE HAND

For people on Earth, the most obvious of these forces—gravity—keeps them planted firmly on the ground. Everyone knows that a person can jump only a few feet into the air by his or her own power. Like a giant invisible hand, gravity pulls the person back down. The amount of downward force that gravity exerts on a person or object is called weight. If you weigh 100 pounds (45 kilograms), gravity is pulling you downward with 100 pounds of force.

This is only the case for people, animals, and objects on Earth's surface. A person who visited the moon could jump six times as high as on Earth. That is because the moon's gravity is only one-sixth as powerful as Earth's.

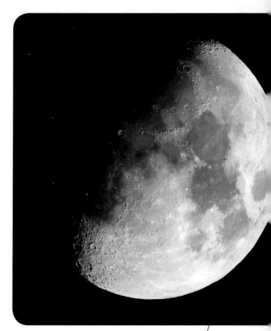

A person who weighs 100 pounds on Earth would only weigh about 17 pounds (7.7 kilograms) on the moon.

## *Why a Weightless Person Has Weight*

Astronauts orbiting Earth are often said to be weightless. The truth is they only feel, or perceive themselves to be, weightless. Earth's gravity still pulls on them, as it does on their spacecraft. They do not plummet downward because they are moving fast enough so that Earth's surface curves away from them at the same rate as their fall. In space, both the astronauts and their craft are in a state of free fall. This gives the astronauts the false impression of having no weight.

On Earth, the perception of weight comes from the force exerted on a person by the ground or floor. When that support is removed, the person goes into free fall and feels weightless.

Skydivers feel weightless for a short time despite gravity's pull on them. When the air resistance is great enough to support the divers, they will not feel weightless, even though they are still falling.

## MASS REMAINS CONSTANT

Weight is relative because it varies from place to place, but mass stays the same. Mass is the amount of matter, or material, an object has. Earth has more mass than the moon, the moon has more mass than a mountain, and a mountain has more mass than an elephant. An object's mass is constant, regardless of whether it is on Earth or the moon. No matter where you travel in the universe, your mass will remain the same.

Mount Fuji, the highest mountain in Japan, is 12,385 feet (3,777 meters) in height. Its mass is the same on Earth as it would be anywhere else in the universe.

The more mass an object has, the larger the gravitational pull. Because Earth has more mass than the moon, Earth has a larger gravitational pull, making things on Earth weigh more. Planets with more mass than Earth have stronger gravities than Earth's. Jupiter, the largest and most massive planet in the solar system, is a good example. If you lived there, you would weigh 2.6 times as much as on Earth. Therefore, someone who weighs 100 pounds on Earth would weigh 260 pounds (416 kg) on Jupiter.

## MASS AND RESISTANCE

Mass can also be measured by its ability to resist outside forces. An object's mass resists a force that acts on it, even when that force makes the object move. Take the example of someone swiftly pulling a tablecloth from underneath some heavy dishes on a tabletop. Although the dishes will move slightly, the mass of the dishes resists the force of the moving cloth so that their change in motion is small. Contact with the tabletop will then quickly stop the dishes. If light paper or plastic plates are used,

**DID YOU KNOW?**

The sun's gravity is about 28 times as strong as Earth's gravity. If a 100-pound person could stand on the sun's surface, he or she would weigh 2,800 pounds (1,260 kg).

the change in motion will be large because of their small mass, and they will most likely end up on the floor.

In the same sense, it is much easier to push a marble than to push a bowling ball to the same speed. The bowling ball has more mass, so more force is needed to get the same change in motion. If the same force is used, the bowling ball will not move as far as the marble.

Moreover, the amount of that resistance is the same

no matter where the ball is. Suppose that astronauts someday build a bowling alley on the moon. A bowler there would be able to pick up a ball more easily because it would weigh only one-sixth as much as it would on Earth. But it would be just as difficult to push the ball along the floor as on Earth. This is because the ball's mass and ability to resist outside forces are the same in both places.

Athletes competing in the high jump try to overcome gravity's pull on their bodies.

# Gravity and Other Universal Forces

**FOR A LONG TIME,** people took gravity for granted. No one knew why an object thrown into the air fell to the ground. Nor did anyone connect this mysterious force to the heavenly bodies far above. No one realized that the force that makes things stay on Earth's surface and the force that governs the movements of the planets are the same.

Gravity, the force that keeps us on Earth, also keeps the planets in our solar system in orbit around the sun.

## INVISIBLE HEAVENLY SPHERES

It took humanity thousands of years to figure out what gravity is and how it works. The ancient Greek scholar Aristotle proposed that each of the heavenly bodies was attached to a giant invisible sphere. He thought each planet moved along the surface of its sphere, and each heavenly sphere nested inside another one. Aristotle claimed there were more than 55 such spheres, all of them encasing Earth, which lay at the center of the universe.

Roman marble bust of the Greek philosopher Aristotle (384–322 B.C.)

But what about the tendency for objects on Earth to fall downward? Aristotle accepted this as the natural way of things. He also assumed that heavy objects fall faster than light ones.

## GALILEO AND FALLING OBJECTS

In the early 1600s, Italian scientist Galileo Galilei took a fresh look at the motion of falling objects. He reasoned that there must be some invisible natural force causing them to

fall. If so, that force would likely pull on all things on Earth equally. From these conclusions, Galileo suspected that Aristotle was wrong about heavy objects falling faster than light ones.

Eager to test his conclusions, Galileo dropped objects of different weights from a great height. He found that all the objects fell at the same rate. Still, Galileo was unable to explain why this happened. Like Aristotle, he did not connect motion in the heavens with motion on Earth.

Galileo used many pieces of equipment—such as a telescope, a magnet, a compass, and a pendulum clock—to study the laws of nature.

## Duplicating Galileo

Galileo's experiment with falling weights can be duplicated with items found around the house. First, find a heavy book and a piece of paper. Trim the paper so it is slightly smaller than the book. Hold the two objects, one in each hand, high above the floor and drop them at the same time. The paper will take longer to hit the floor.

However, this does not mean Galileo was wrong. The reason the paper takes longer to drop is that it encounters air resistance on the way down. The book also encounters air resistance, but it is heavy enough that the air resistance has little effect on it.

To eliminate the air pressure factor, place the paper on top of the book and drop them both. This time, both objects will fall in unison, confirming what Galileo proved five centuries ago.

Galileo Galilei (1564–1642) was an Italian astronomer, mathematician, and physicist. His diverse knowledge allowed him to experiment across many fields of science.

## THE APPLE AND THE MOON

English scientist Isaac Newton was the first person to realize that both kinds of motion—on Earth and in space—have the same cause. According to legend, one day he saw an apple fall from a tree. It occurred to him that the force that Earth exerts on the apple might be the same force Earth exerts on the moon.

Newton also thought that all objects have a measurable amount of mass. The force of gravity that acts on an object depends on its mass. Something small, such as a book or shoe, has very little mass, so very little gravity acts on it. But something as large as a planet has a large amount of mass, so its gravitational pull is large enough to hold people, buildings, and moons in place. In addition, Newton showed that the force of gravity exerted on an object by another object grows weaker as the distance between the two increases.

Isaac Newton (1642–1727) correctly viewed gravity as a property not only of Earth, but of all objects in the universe.

## EINSTEIN AND CURVED SPACE

Newton's theory of gravity revolutionized modern science. However, a later scientist was not completely satisfied with it. Newton had described gravity as a force exerted between objects. Working in the early years of the 20th century, German scientist Albert Einstein proposed a different view.

Albert Einstein (1879–1955), among piles of papers, various books, and a portrait of Isaac Newton, worked on his scientific theories in his study in Berlin, Germany.

Einstein believed that gravity is actually a property of space itself. He claimed that space has a sort of elastic fabric that people cannot see or touch. According to Einstein, planets, moons, and other objects sink into this fabric, creating gravity wells, or depressions. The more mass an object has, the deeper the gravity well it creates and the more space curves.

In Einstein's version of gravity, the moon is drawn toward Earth because the smaller body rolls down into Earth's gravity well. Because the moon is traveling at a high rate of speed, it keeps spinning around inside the well. But if for some reason it suddenly slowed, it would roll farther downward into the well and crash into Earth.

## FOUR UNIVERSAL FORCES

Although gravity is the best-known universal force, scientists have identified three others: electromagnetic, strong nuclear, and weak nuclear. The electromagnetic force binds atoms together to form molecules. Meanwhile, the strong and weak nuclear forces hold together the tiny particles

### DID YOU KNOW?

Of the four universal forces, the strong nuclear force is the strongest, while gravity is the weakest.

that make up the atoms.

Without these three forces, animals, people, mountains, oceans, planets, and stars could not form. No objects would exist to bend space, creating gravity.

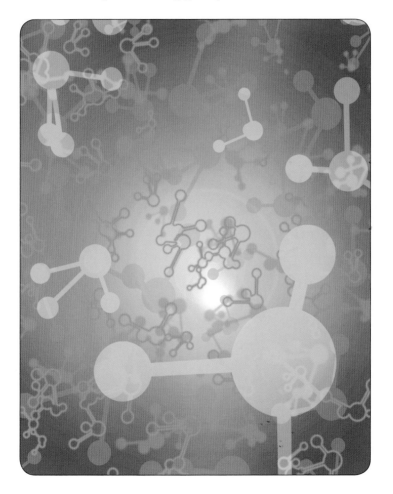

All of the atoms and molecules in the universe are governed by the four universal forces.

# The Laws of Motion

**IN ADDITION TO IDENTIFYING** the universal laws of gravity, Isaac Newton thought there must also be closely related laws that govern how objects move. He later developed three laws explaining the motion of objects everywhere.

Newton published his three laws of motion, along with his theory of gravity, in 1687. His book, titled *Mathematical Principles of Natural Philosophy* (or *Principia* for short), revolutionized science. It showed that the universe is like a vast machine with many parts that move and interact in consistent, predictable, and measurable ways.

### THE FIRST LAW AND INERTIA

Newton's first law states that an object at rest will stay at rest and that an object in motion will stay in motion with the same speed and in the same direction unless acted on by an outside force. This law describes how objects start moving.

Newton proposed that some kind of force must

Once a paintball is shot out of a gun, gravity will pull it down slightly. Otherwise, the paintball will travel in a straight path until it comes into contact with a person, a target, or the ground.

push or pull an object for the object to move. Otherwise, the object would remain motionless. Newton said that all objects have a tendency to resist forces that begin acting on them. He called this tendency inertia and showed that it is directly related to mass. The more massive the object, the more inertia the object possesses and the harder it is to move.

Newton also pointed out that once a force gets an object

A dogsled will remain stationary until a team of dogs pulls on its ropes with enough force to start the sled in motion.

## The Mysterious Spinning Egg

An easy way to see Newton's first law in action is to place a fresh egg on its side on a smooth countertop. With your fingers, make the egg spin around like a top. Then gently stop it with one finger and quickly remove the finger. The egg will suddenly start moving again before eventually stopping.

This mysterious motion occurs because spinning the egg set both the shell and the liquid interior in motion. Your finger stopped the shell, but the liquid inside kept moving, causing the shell to start moving again until the friction of the countertop finally caused both the shell and the liquid to stop.

moving, the object still has inertia. The inertia will resist change and try to keep the object in its existing state, whether it is moving or motionless. Therefore, the object will continue to move in the same direction and at the same speed unless a second force acts on it.

One force that can alter the speed of a moving object is friction. Friction opposes the motions of objects that slide against each other. To test how friction can slow down a moving object, try shoving a book along a tabletop. Not surprisingly, the book quickly slows and stops. The friction between the book and the tabletop causes the book to stop moving.

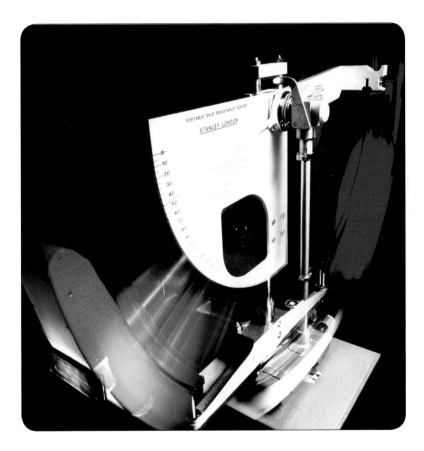

## THE SECOND LAW OF MOTION

Moving the book across the tabletop also illustrates Newton's second law of motion, which states that a force acting on an object will do one of three things. It might accelerate it (speed it up), decelerate it (slow it down), or change the direction in which the object is moving.

A friction tester can determine the slipperiness of floor tiles. A pendulum sweeps across the floor tile, losing momentum at each contact because of friction. A scale then measures the lost momentum.

In the case of the book, pushing it causes it to briefly accelerate across the table-top. If you do the same with a heavier book, you will need to exert more force to move it the same distance as the lighter book. Regardless of which book is being pushed, a second force comes into play. The friction exerted by the tabletop opposes each book's motion.

## THE THIRD LAW OF MOTION

Newton explained his third law of motion this way: "For every action, there is an equal and opposite reaction." In this case, the word action refers to a force on an object, and reaction refers to the simultaneous force the object exerts in return. These actions and reactions are equal in strength and act in opposite directions.

In hockey, the puck will glide along the ice until acted upon by an outside force, such as a hockey player changing the puck's direction or friction from the ice slowing it down.

Forces never occur alone; they always occur in action-and-reaction pairs.

One of the best-known examples of Newton's third law can be seen when someone lets the air out of a balloon. The force of the balloon pushing air out is accompanied by the force of the air pushing the balloon in the opposite direction.

Squids use Newton's third law to move through the sea. The squid takes in water, and then shoots it toward its rear. The backward force of the water is accompanied by the forward force on the squid.

The same thing happens with a rocket. The rocket exerts a backward force on the hot gases blasting from the back of the rocket. At the same time, the hot gases exert an equal force on the rocket, but in the opposite direction. As a result, the rocket hurtles upward and the gases blast away in the other direction.

Scientists and engineers use the third law of motion to launch rockets into space.

## Energy and Speed ⊕

**NEWTON'S DISCOVERIES** about mass, forces, and motion led to many more scientific advances. Later researchers learned that the basic laws of the physical world are involved in the production of energy. In a general sense, energy is the ability or potential to cause change. Whenever a force changes the energy of something, the amount of energy change is called work.

Many forms of energy exist. When you climb out of bed in the morning, you use chemical energy stored in your muscles to create

A leaf-cutter ant is capable of a large amount of work. It can haul food and other objects that are many times its size and weight back to its nest.

mechanical energy in your motion. In the kitchen you use electrical energy to turn on the toaster, which then creates heat energy to toast bread. When you eat the toast, your body converts some of it to chemical energy when you digest it. Light energy allows you to see, while sound energy carries your family's conversation to your ears. Almost all of the energy we use or experience every day can be traced back to nuclear energy from the sun.

A typical morning involves many types of energy.

## Mass into Energy

Mass is a form of energy. An object's mass is sometimes known as "frozen energy" that can, under certain conditions, be converted into other forms of energy. This is what occurs inside the sun. Every second, reactions in the sun cause a small portion of an object's mass to be converted into heat and light energy.

Even a tiny quantity of mass has the potential to create huge amounts of energy. Imagine if the mass contained in a baseball (145 grams; 5 ounces) could be converted to energy. That energy would propel a car forward at 65 miles (104 km) per hour for 5,000 years!

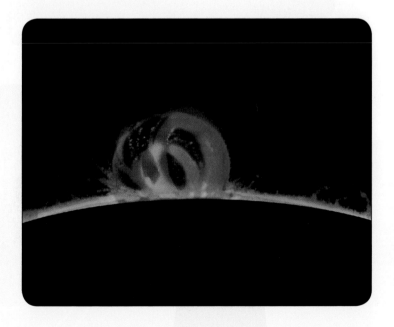

Solar flares on the sun erupt with bursts of energy equal to millions of hydrogen bombs.

## WORKING ENERGY VERSUS STORED ENERGY

Scientists divide all forms of energy into two broad categories. The first, kinetic energy, can be thought of as "moving" energy. Moving objects can cause great changes. The more motion there is, the greater the possible changes.

The other kind of energy, potential energy, can be thought of as "stored" energy. Many objects contain potential energy that is waiting to be released and converted into other forms of energy, such as kinetic energy.

For example, a roller coaster car that has reached the highest point in the ride is filled with potential energy. When

A horse pulling a cart possesses kinetic energy. The energy exerted by the horse creates forward motion, moving both the horse and cart, and thereby accomplishing work.

## POTENTIAL AND KINETIC ENERGY

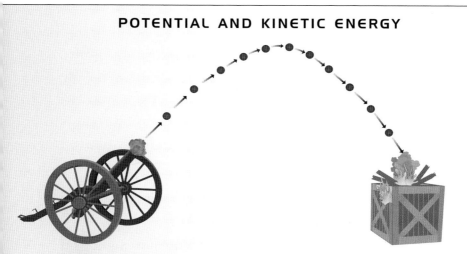

The explosion that shoots a cannonball out of a cannon possesses kinetic energy. As the cannonball travels upward, the kinetic energy converts to potential energy. At the peak, the cannonball only has potential energy. As the cannonball begins to fall, the potential energy converts back to kinetic energy until it strikes the ground or target.

the car rolls downward, the potential energy is released in the form of kinetic energy. A single roller coaster ride goes through many energy conversions, or changes. Kinetic energy converts into potential energy and vice versa, over and over again.

To demonstrate the conversion of potential energy into kinetic energy, find a rubber band, grasp one end, and stretch it back. The stretched band contains plenty of potential energy. Now let go and watch as the potential energy converts into kinetic energy, sending the band flying across the room.

## COMMON ENERGY CONVERSIONS

Another energy conversion occurs when you shoot a rubber band. Take a fresh rubber band and press it to your lips. It will be room temperature. Then shoot the band several times and touch it to your lips again. It will be noticeably warmer. This is because some of the stored energy in the band was converted into heat energy.

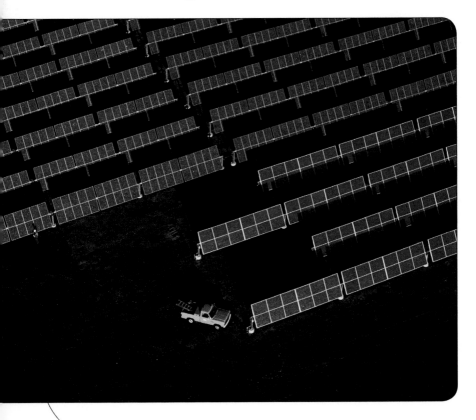

Solar panels collect energy from sunlight, which is then converted into electricity.

Any form of energy can be converted into other forms of energy. These conversions occur all around us. Windmills convert the kinetic energy of wind into electrical energy. Chemical energy in gasoline is converted to heat energy when the gasoline burns. In an engine, heat energy can be converted into mechanical energy in the form of gears turning.

A device known as Newton's cradle illustrates a form of energy conversion. From a lifted position, the ball on the left has potential energy. Once the ball is let go, kinetic energy from the impact transfers through the other balls, causing the right ball to swing upward and gain potential energy. The process will continue until friction and gravity bring the balls to a stop.

All of these energy conversions follow a simple but important natural law: Energy can neither be created nor destroyed. Also, when an energy conversion takes place, no energy is lost. The amount of heat energy produced in burning gasoline will be the same as the amount of chemical energy in the unburned gasoline. Scientists call this rule the Law of Conservation of Energy.

## HOW SPEED AFFECTS ENERGY

The Law of Conservation of Energy applies when a moving car crashes into a brick wall. At the moment of impact, most of the car's kinetic energy is converted to heat energy. Much of the heat energy stays in the car, but some of it is transferred into the wall. The energy not converted to heat goes into sound energy and into damage to the car and wall. The amount of heat plus this sound and damage equal the kinetic energy that was possessed by the moving car.

However, the amount of kinetic energy converted to heat

**DID YOU KNOW?**

Nature sets a maximum speed limit known as the speed of light: 186,000 miles (about 300,000 kilometers) per second. Objects with mass cannot be accelerated to light speed.

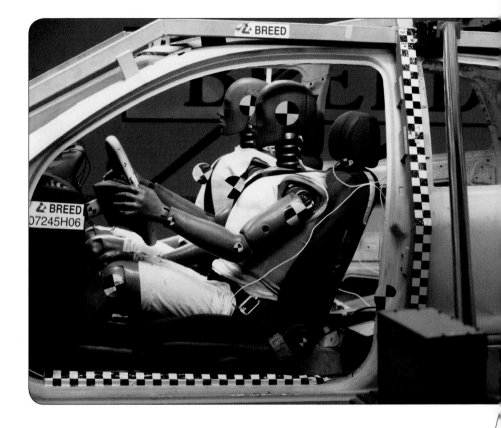

energy during the crash depends on the car's speed. The faster an object moves, the more energy it has. When a moving object's speed doubles, its kinetic energy increases four times. A car traveling at 60 miles (96 km) per hour will crash into a wall with four times as much energy as a car moving at 30 miles (48 km) per hour. That is one reason high-speed car crashes are much more destructive than low-speed crashes.

Because so much energy is involved in a crash, car companies test their vehicles before putting them on the market. Crash-test dummies simulate what would happen to people in a crash.

# CHAPTER FIVE

# Pressure and Floating Bodies

**GRAVITY AND FRICTION** are forces that people experience every day. Another force, pressure, is also common. Scientists define pressure as the amount of force an object exerts over a certain area.

Consider what happens if you walk through a deep snowbank.

If you are wearing ordinary shoes, your foot will sink deep into the snow with each step. Because all of your weight is concentrated in a small area, your weight pushes downward with great pressure.

On the other hand, if you put on a pair of snowshoes, you will sink less than an inch into the snow. A snowshoe is much wider and longer than an ordinary shoe, so it distributes your weight over a bigger area. That reduces the pressure you exert on each square inch of snow.

Snowshoes are used to spread the pressure from a person's body weight over a greater area, allowing the person to walk on deep snow without sinking very far.

## FLOATING AND SINKING

People create varying amounts of pressure not only by walking, but also by sitting, lying down, or touching things. Liquids exert pressure, too. When someone swims near the ocean's surface, the water exerts a safe amount of pressure on the person's body. However, if someone tried to swim a mile beneath the surface, the water above the person would press down with enormous force and damage the swimmer's body.

Scuba divers can swim approximately 330 feet (100 meters) below sea level before the pressure on their bodies from the water reaches unsafe levels.

## WATER PRESSURE

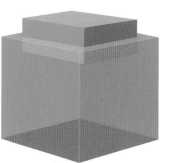

If an object has less weight than an equal volume of water, differences in the water's pressure over the surface of the object buoy it up, so it floats.

If an object has more weight than an equal volume of water, it overcomes these pressure differences and sinks.

The pressure exerted by liquids also causes objects to be buoyant (meaning they float) and to sink. More than 2,000 years ago, the Greek scientist Archimedes (287–212 B.C.) discovered the principle of buoyancy. He showed that an object placed in water displaces some of the water. The weight of the water that is displaced equals the weight of the object itself.

## FLOATING AND FLYING IN AIR

Pressure works in a similar manner in the air. A balloon filled with helium gas rises and floats in the air. The helium inside is lighter than an equal amount of air on the outside, so air pressure pushes the balloon upward. Air pressure also makes it possible for airplanes to fly.

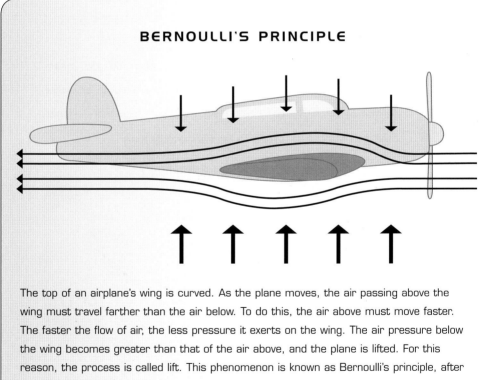

# BERNOULLI'S PRINCIPLE

The top of an airplane's wing is curved. As the plane moves, the air passing above the wing must travel farther than the air below. To do this, the air above must move faster. The faster the flow of air, the less pressure it exerts on the wing. The air pressure below the wing becomes greater than that of the air above, and the plane is lifted. For this reason, the process is called lift. This phenomenon is known as Bernoulli's principle, after Daniel Bernoulli (1700–1782), a Swiss scientist.

## Why Fish Do Not Sink

A bony fish remains buoyant in water because its body contains a swim bladder, a sac containing air. The swim bladder works because of differences in density, which is the relationship of an object's mass to its volume. An object with a lot of mass in a given volume is denser than an object with less mass in the same volume. For example, air is less dense than water because there are fewer air molecules in a given volume than water molecules in that volume.

In the case of the fish, the air in the swim bladder makes the fish's body weigh the same as an equal volume of water. Because the force of water pressure equals the fish's weight, the fish is neither forced to surface nor to sink.

A fish can swim without sinking or floating to the top because its total body weight is the same density as the surrounding water.

# CHAPTER SIX

# Simple and Complex Machines

**HUMAN CIVILIZATION** was built with machines. In ancient times, most machines were simple, while today many are very complex.

However, all machines have certain things in common. First, they increase the usefulness of natural forces. Second, all machines work by exerting a small amount of force over a relatively large distance. This produces the same effect as a large amount of force applied over a short distance. Therefore, the effort required to accomplish a task is reduced significantly.

A nail gun uses compressed air to drive a nail into the wall. This requires much less work from the person than a traditional hammer would.

## RAMPS AND WEDGES

Consider how the ancient Egyptians used one of the simplest
machines: the inclined plane, or ramp. An inclined plane
allows workers to partially overcome gravity's pull on heavy

The ancient Egyptians used simple machines while constructing the pyramids.

objects. To build their immense pyramids, the Egyptians had to lift many heavy stone blocks to a great height. But lifting a block straight up required a huge amount of effort by many workers. The builders overcame this difficulty by constructing ramps around the sides of the pyramid. Though the distance a block moved was now much farther, less effort and fewer workers were needed to drag the block along the ramps.

Another version of the inclined plane, the wedge, magnifies forces instead of reducing them. A metal wedge is commonly used in splitting firewood. Someone hits the wedge with a hammer, driving the wedge downward into the wood. The wedge converts the downward force applied by the hammer into a much greater sideways force. As a result, the wood splits apart.

## OTHER SIMPLE MACHINES

The lever is another simple machine that makes work easier. A lever consists of a long bar that turns or pivots on a stationary point called the fulcrum. One of the more familiar tools that uses the lever is the wheelbarrow. In this case, the fulcrum is the axle at the center of the wheelbarrow's wheel. The closer an object is placed to the wheel of the wheelbarrow, the greater the distance to the wheelbarrow's handles. It is then easier to lift the handles and move the object.

## COMPLEX MACHINES

Over time, human inventors learned to combine several kinds of simple machines in complex ways. Examples include bicycles, clocks, windmills, typewriters, sewing machines, elevators, and cars. A car combines many types of simple machines—including wheels and axles, gears, and levers. The result is a single, complex machine that manipulates natural forces to produce movement. In this way, complex machines will become even more enhanced as people continue to explore the laws of nature that govern the universe.

A moving dolly uses the same basic principles of a wheelbarrow. Heavy objects are placed near the wheel (fulcrum), so less effort is required to lift and move them.

## How Gears Transmit Forces

The gear—a variation of the wheel—features evenly spaced notches, or teeth, along a wheel's rim. When the notches of a turning gear interlock with a second gear, the force generated by the first gear is transmitted to the second, making the second gear turn. Gears of varying sizes can be used to transmit, magnify, and reduce forces.

Gears can also change the direction of forces. When you place a gear at a right angle to another, the teeth of the gears interlock, and the force generated by the first gear changes direction by 90 degrees.

Tiny gears are used to make up the intricate mechanisms in a clock or watch.

These universal laws include those involving forces and motion. Try to imagine life without them. Without gravity, for example, people and other objects would float off Earth aimlessly into space. Without pushing, pulling, and the movement and work that result from them, life would be motionless and boring. Therefore, forces and motion make life as we know it possible.

Forces and motion make the world an exciting place to live.

accelerate—to move steadily faster

Bernoulli's principle—natural phenomenon in which faster-moving air exerts less pressure on a surface than slower-moving air

buoyancy—natural phenomenon that occurs when a submerged object is less dense than the water and is pushed up by water pressure, making it float

conversion—process of changing one substance or form of energy into another

decelerate—to move steadily slower

density—relationship of an object's mass to its volume

friction—force that impedes the motion of two objects as they slide against each other

fulcrum—stationary point on which a lever pivots

gravity wells—depressions in the fabric of space created by the mass of an object; the more massive the object, the deeper the well

inertia—tendency of an object to remain either at rest or in motion unless affected by an outside force

kinetic energy—energy, or work accomplished, by a moving object

lift—mechanical force that opposes or overcomes the weight of a bird or airplane, allowing both to fly

mass—amount of matter, or material, contained in an object

potential energy—energy stored within an object, waiting to be released

pressure—amount of force an object exerts per unit of area

▶ Earth's mass was first calculated in 1798 by English researcher Henry Cavendish. He suspended a small lead ball and a larger lead ball from wires. Then he measured tiny movements caused by the gravitational attraction between the balls. This showed how much objects of different masses attract each other at a given distance. Cavendish applied what he had learned to Earth. Using one of Newton's formulas, he calculated Earth's mass to be 6 sextillion (6 billion trillion) tons. This value is only about 1 percent off the amount calculated by scientists in the 20th century.

▶ Galileo observed how arrows, cannonballs, and other projectiles move. When an archer fires an arrow, Galileo said, the arrow moves forward, but it also moves upward and then downward. The combination of the two motions traces out a curved path called a parabola.

▶ When planning rocket launchings, scientists take Newton's second law of motion into account. That law tells them that the force produced by the rocket's engines will accelerate the rocket upward into the sky. The same law predicts that the amount of acceleration depends on the rocket's mass. A lighter rocket will accelerate more. So as the rocket uses up its fuel and becomes lighter, its acceleration increases.

▶ Moving objects possess momentum, defined as mass multiplied by speed. A very massive object, such as a truck, has a lot of momentum when traveling at 30 miles (48 km) per hour, whereas a softball, with much less mass, has far less momentum when traveling at that same speed.

Because they can reach speeds up to 70 miles (112 km) per hour, cheetahs have great momentum even though they do not have a large amount of mass.

## At the Library

Dispezio, Michael A. *Awesome Experiments in Force & Motion.*
New York: Sterling Publishing, 1998.
Lafferty, Peter. *Force & Motion.* New York: Dorling Kindersley,
1999.
Riley, Peter. *Forces and Movement.* North Mankato, Minn.:
Smart Apple Media, 2006.

## On the Web

For more information on this subject, use Facthound.
1. Go to *www.facthound.com*
2. Type in this book ID: 0756532647
3. Click on the Fetch It button.
Facthound will find the best Web sites for you.

## On the Road

Boston Museum of Science
Science Park
Boston, MA 02114
617/723-2500

Chicago Museum of Science
and Industry
57th Street and Lake Shore Drive
Chicago, IL 60637-2093
773/684-1414

## Explore all the Physical Science books

Atoms & Molecules: Building Blocks
of the Universe

Chemical Change: From Fireworks
to Rust

Electrical Circuits: Harnessing
Electricity

Force and Motion: Laws of
Movement

Kinetic Energy: The Energy of
Motion

Manipulating Light: Reflection,
Refraction, and Absorption

The Periodic Table: Mapping the
Elements

Physical Change: Reshaping Matter

Waves: Energy on the Move

A complete list of Exploring Science titles is available
on our Web site: *www.compasspointbooks.com*